# HUNGARY

Essay by Gyula Fekete • 237 colour plates • Corvina

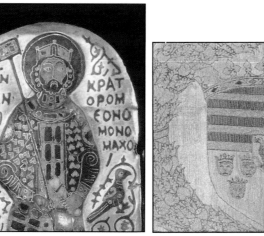

**H**ungary is a country of encounters, a country of conflicts. Her geographical situation has almost predestined the land and the peoples who settled here to this fate. In this land, even the forces of nature clash and fight for hegemony. From the northwest, the oceanic air currents break into the Carpathian Basin, taking a roundabout way because of the Alps; those of the Mediterranean arrive from the south and the continental influences from east or southeast. Now one wins, now the other—the Hungarian meteorologist can never be sure of himself. None of these influences can conquer the land for good, and none of them withdraws defeated for good; the surrounding climatic zones have been struggling for thousands of years for possession of the Carpathian Basin, each from its own position of strength.

Hungary is a historical crossway, too. Here, the highroads of many peoples meet. Today's highways and the lines of the twenty express trains that cross Budapest can be traced back two thousand years. The two important transcontinental-intercontinental roads of the Roman age, the Silk Road, which connected the West and the East, and the north-to-south Amber Road which connected Italy and the Baltic, met in Transdanubia.

Yet not only roads that connect peoples passed through this land but also *fronts* that separate peoples, and this also for thousands of years: at least since the watch-towers were built along the *limes* of the Roman Empire to hold back the incessant, formidable attacks of barbaric tribes along the Danube.

One can hardly count how many times the region of the middle course of the Danube has been the battlefield of East and West; how many times the Romans, Huns, Avars, Magyars, Mongols, Turks, Germanic and Slavic peoples—or if you prefer, civilized and barbaric, pagan and Christian, Catholic and Protestant, revolutionary and anti-revolutionary, Magyar and Magyar—have clashed on the banks of the Danube.

The land has been inhabited since ancient times. Traces of one of the oldest European settlements, estimated to be half a million years old, were found in the Vértes mountains in Transdanubia. Primitive man dwelt in the caves of its karstic regions; then came the thousands of years of nomadic tribes. But no really significant culture had developed until the Roman conquest. Part of the territory of Hungary then became a province of the Roman Empire under the name Pannonia. Afterwards, the waves of invaders swept away the province of Pannonia, together with the traces of the Sarmatians, Gepids and Celts; Huns, Ostrogoths, Longobards, Avars chased each other across the land, Slavic tribes settled down here, and as long as the Frankish Empire remained strong, incursions from the west also reached the land.

The *Magyar Conquest*—so we call the last years of the ninth century when the Magyar confederacy of tribes, with an army of 108 families, invaded the Carpathian Basin. But the most difficult undertaking was yet to come—permanent settlement on this draughty land to establish an independent state.

The flow of peoples from the East continued: the Cumans broke in, then Mongolian hordes raided the country, killing and enslaving its inhabitants. Those who were lucky enough to come through could begin to sow the land anew and, rid of the Eastern danger for a time, to set

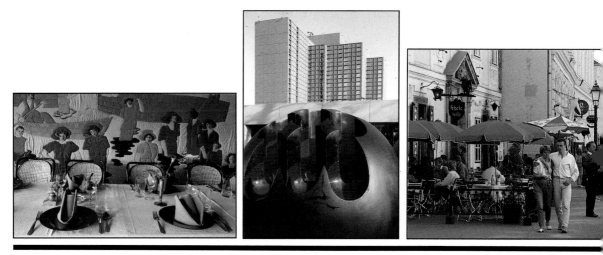

about struggling with the Western danger.
By the time the country had recovered from
the devastation of the Mongolian invasion, a new
threat was near: the Turks. First we beat them,
then they beat us and became the masters of the
greater part of the country for a century and a half.
As soon as the Turks had been ousted came
the struggle for independence—from the West.
The alliance between the Habsburgs, the local
aristocracy and the Catholic clergy gave us a semi-
colonial state for four centuries. Even though we
sometimes succeeded in tearing at the leash,
the country was only liberated from Austro-
German subordination by the Soviet Union when
it overpowered Fascism.
We may well be the people who have seen
the hardest times in Europe. Always serving as
the ground of the struggles between the forces
of the East and West, we have dwindled to the
present small people of ten million, although even
after a catastrophe such as the Mongolian
devastation (1241–1242), we had as many
inhabitants as England.
In this stormy corner of Europe, in the graveyard
of so many ancient and medieval peoples, bare
survival itself required an incredible toughness.
And this was something more than a mere instinct
for life, for there were times when we were
in the forefront of human progress. For in
the epoch of the science and art-loving Hunyadis
who momentarily defeated the Turks, or at the
time of the War of Independence in 1848–1849, or
during the 1918–1919 revolution, we, too, made
world history.
Today we are among the pioneers again; again
this means struggle and enormous sacrifices.
We are trying to create something new; something
which will be valid not only for us but for other
peoples, too. We are confident that history will
justify us again.

There is something which cannot clearly be seen
in the photographs. Namely, that we were born
to this earth not entirely without luck; to this land
which is not too rich to make her sons slack, nor
so bare that they must live in distress. The country
is not so large that we cannot sense its boundaries
in all directions, nor is it so small as not to provide
space for even the greatest creative impulse.
It is not the home of over-refined culture that has
lost touch with reality, nor is it that of a primitive
people isolated from its time.
It is neither very much like this, nor very much like
that, and yet, there is nothing we have been so far
from as the *golden mean.* We are a country
of extremes, often of extreme ambitions. We have
given the world hangmen and heroes, brilliant
minds and dull men of power, men of success,
and consumptives dying before their prime, fine
love lyrics, and prostitutes.
Nor will the photographs show clearly enough that
there is hardly a people on the earth who yearn
for global reconciliation more earnestly
than we.
So far we have been a bumper—the third party
which held back assailants from two directions
and received the blows they directed at each other.
We want to become that which we are predestined
to be by our historical-geographical situation:
*a bridge* between points of the compass,
and a *link* between trends and peoples who are
reconciled with one another for good.
Only this role and vocation can compensate
us for our history.

# BUDAPEST

T he main artery is the Danube, and on its banks is the pulsating heart of the country, Budapest. I would call it the *athletic heart* of the country, and since the town is a great sports center, this is doubly appropriate.

Budapest is the capital of two million inhabitants, in a country of ten million people, which means that every fifth person lives here. And if we add the number of those who earn their living in the capital, it is clear that the fate of one-fourth of the population is linked with Budapest, mainly through industry.

As a settlement, Budapest is thousands of years old, especially Buda with its hills and valleys abounding in caves. For centuries it has been the center of the country, its royal seat, and capital. But it was ruined and rebuilt so many times that it appears much younger. The taste of our great-grandfathers has left clearer traces on the townscape than if it had been refined by centuries of peace. What is now *old* in Budapest was born after the Turkish occupation, built in the eighteenth-nineteenth century Neo-Classical style, the late Baroque, Eclecticism, and Art Nouveau. After the devastations of World War II, these buildings have been reconstructed in their original form.

An exception is the Castle District, which was so thoroughly ruined, and was in need of such drastic renovation, that the medieval architectural elements previously hidden behind the new façades were revealed, and thereafter preserved. As a consequence, the district as it now stands bears closer resemblance to the original than almost any other part of the town.

But modern architecture is also present in the Budapest townscape, and it is becoming more and more prominent. There are whole districts of new houses, institutions and hotels along the Danube.

However, it is not just the buildings that make Budapest beautiful. For this city is not simply beautiful: it is enchanting. Impartial travelers count it among the most beautiful cities in the world. What makes it enchanting is the joint work of nature and man.

Let us take the Danube. It is not a little river that gets lost among a sea of houses, but a vast waterway, flowing with royal dignity, a permanent ambassador of nature accredited to a series of capitals. Or take Gellért Hill. If it were higher, it would break up the town around it, upset its proportions and rule over man's works with oppressive superiority. Instead, it harmonizes perfectly with the rest of the townscape; its bold rise and robust rocks radiate grandeur and strength, but the joint works of nature and man have put it in scale with the bigger but more distant Buda hills.

The above reveals only as much of the presence of nature as any picture postcard can document. The invisible depth of the hills has also been penetrated by nature and man. Budapest is the richest capital in caves and medicinal waters; from its 123 natural and artificial springs, 70 million liters of thermal water gush forth a day. There is a separate nature conservation area in the middle of the town, the Sas-hegy, a meeting-point of the Mediterranean and steppe flora. And if we add the squirrels, tits, blackbirds, foxes, deer, and rabbits that inhabit the immediate surroundings of the city, it will perhaps turn out that Budapest is the most densely populated capital in this respect, too.

In the foreground,
the Fishermen's Bastion,
in the background,
in Pest, the Parliament.

Reminders of the Roman Age:
ruins of the military amphitheater
in Óbuda. At one time,
it accommodated 15 thousand
spectators. Floor mosaic
in the Hercules Villa
in Meggyfa utca.

One of the beautiful pieces
displayed in the Museum of
Budapest's History. The statues
dating from the House of Anjou
are probably from the court of
Sigismund of Luxemburg
(1368–1437). The Gothic *sedilia*
are in one of the medieval houses
of the Castle District.

The Király Baths was built by
Sokoli Mustapha in the 16th
century. The miniature is from
a Turkish codex of 1588: the
Sultan surveys the siege of the
castle of Buda.

The southern Great Bastion
of the restored medieval castle
wall.

The Lion Gate.

Buda Castle. Inset: one of
Baroque gates.

The construction of Buda Castle on Castle Hill was begun
after the Mongolian invasion in the mid-13th century by
King Béla IV. The famous Gothic and Renaissance palace
was built in the 14th and 15th centuries during the reign of
Sigismund of Luxemburg and King Matthias Corvinus. It
was destroyed for the first time in 1686, when after the
Turkish occupation it was besieged by united European
forces. The Baroque palace was built after the siege.
Another siege followed during the freedom fights of 1849,
which in turn was followed by rebuilding and expansion.
But the greatest damage of all came in 1945, during the
Second World War, when the castle was reduced to a pile
of stones. On the other hand, this devastation led to the dis-
covery of the medieval treasures and traces of the old
buildings buried deep under ground. Today, the restored
royal palace is not the seat of political power, but a cultural
center comprising several museums, including the National Gallery and the National Széchényi Library, the largest
public library in the country.

14

The crown of St. Stephen (1000–1038), the first king of Hungary, is the symbol of the country's statehood. Taken to the U.S. in 1945, the crown was returned to Hungary in 1978 and displayed at the Hungarian National Museum.

Bertalan Székely (1835–1910): *The Women of Eger*, 1867. Mihály Munkácsy (1844–1900): *Linen Shredding*, 1871.

16

19

László Mednyánszky (1862–1919): *Head of a Vagabond,* 1897.

József Rippl-Rónai (1861–1927): *Woman with a Black Veil,* 1896.

The Hungarian National Gallery
is in the rebuilt Royal Palace.
It is devoted to Hungarian art.

Károly Ferenczy (1862–1917): *October,* 1903.

Lajos Gulácsy (1882–1932): *Paolo and Francesca,* 1903.

20

Tárnok utca 14–16: medieval merchants' houses in the Castle District. The façade of the house at No. 14 is covered with 16th century wall painting.

Detail of the Neo-Baroque facade of the house at Úri utca 58.

Vienna Gate Square, the location of the former Saturday Market.

Yard of the house at Országház utca 16.

Terrace of the Hilton Hotel
in the Castle District. The ruins
of a Dominican church and
monastery have been
incorporated into the modern
design.

Two towers
in Táncsics Mihály utca:
that of the Hilton
and Matthias Church.

Országház utca.
In the 15th century, this was
the main thoroughfare
of the Castle District.

Medieval stone-ledge
at Országház utca 20.

29

The Matthias Church, formerly known as the Church of Our Lady, was founded over seven hundred years ago by King Béla IV (1235–1270). After several reconstructions, it gained its present aspect at the end of the 19th century.

The equestrian statue of St. Stephen, the first king of Hungary.

Towers of the Matthias Church and Fishermen's Bastion.

30

The southern tip of the island
with sunbathers.

Like a huge, two-thirds of a kilometer long, five hundred
meters wide ship, Margaret Island stands on the Danube
wedged in between Pest and Buda. Its two-thousand-
year-old history is preserved by several ruins – Roman age
watch towers, the remnants of a medieval cloister, and
latter-day summer homes. Today it is one of the largest
parks of the capital with beautiful gardens where flowers
are planted to suit the seasons of the year.

The twelve-story high
water tower, today a protected
industrial monument.

These vehicles do not pollute
the air of the island.

The Chain Bridge, the oldest
bridge in the capital, with the new
hotel row in the background.

The Chain Bridge was built
on the initiative of Count
István Széchenyi, the greatest figure
of the 19th century Reform Age.
Designed by the English engineer
William Thierney Clark, it was
constructed under the direction of
Adam Clark. Blown up in the Second
World War, it was re-inaugurated in
1949, which also marked the one
hundredth anniversary of its
initial opening.

Francis Joseph (today Liberty)
Bridge was built for the Millennial
celebrations marking Hungary's
one thousand years of statehood.

As Gyula Krúdy, the great early twentieth-century writer
phrased it, "We all have our own visions of Heaven. The
men of Óbuda, for example, have had the fixed idea since
1867 that the road to Heaven leads over a bridge which
spans the Danube. . ." Well, the long-awaited Árpád Bridge
which touched the northern tip of Margaret Island was built
at last – the longest bridge in Central Europe – yet nothing
could take the glory away from Széchenyi's Chain Bridge,
the first of the light bridges to be built connecting Pest and
Buda. It's not as wide as the others, nor as long or as
crowded, yet even in its present reconstructed form (it was
blown up by the Germans during the Second World War), it
has an atmosphere of nostalgia; it is the embodiment of
Budapest's history.
The area once encircled by the city wall on the Pest side of
the Danube is today's Inner City.

Elizabeth Bridge spans
the Danube in one graceful sweep.

On Váci utca.

Siesta after
a tiring
Inner City tour.

Today, the most characteristic street of the Inner City is Váci utca. But its character comes not so much from its past as its present. Dotted with fashionable shops, it is a pedestrian street closed to traffic.

Hotel Taverna in the heart
of the Inner City.

The statue of the great 19th century
poet, Mihály Vörösmarty,
made of Carrara marble, stands
in the center of Vörösmarty,
formerly Theater Square.

Modern string of shops
in Régiposta utca.

45

The so-called Paris Arcade inside
the Art Nouveau building on the
corner of Felszabadulás Square.

The Baroque ornaments
of Café Hungaria, the former
New York Café, have been restored
to their original splendor.
At the turn of the century,
the café was frequented
by the writers and artists of Budapest.

46

The building of the former
Postal Savings Bank, today's
National Bank, was designed
by Ödön Lechner. With its majolica
ornaments, made by the famous
Zsolnay porcelain factory,
it is one of the outstanding pieces
of Hungarian Art Nouveau
architecture.

The Danubius Well on Erzsébet Square.

Art Nouveau decoration
on a house on Bajcsy-Zsilinszky út.

50

The National Opera House,
one of the most beautiful
buildings
in the capital, was designed
by Miklós Ybl in Neo-Renaissance
style and built between 1875 and
1884. The most prestigeous
institution of classical music,
it has trained generations
of musicians, conductors
and composers, and has invited great
musicians from all over the world
to give performances.

The auditorium
of the Opera House is decorated
by the frescoes of the best known
19th century artists.

51

The building of Parliament is
a symbol of Hungary's statehood.
The National Assembly first met
here in 1896, the time of the
Millennial celebrations. Its dome
is 96 meters high, its width is 118,
and its length is 268 meters.
It was built after designs
by architect Imre Steindl. Today,
it houses the National Assembly,
the Council of Ministers,
and the Parliamentary Library.

The ornate main staircase
of Parliament.

54

Diego Velazquez (1599–1660):
*Peasants at Table,* 1617–1618.

Pieter Bruegel, the Elder (*c.* 1530–1569):
*The Preaching
of St. John the Baptist,* 1566.

55

Raphaello Santi (1483–1520):
*The Portrait of Pietro Bembo
as a Young Man,* c. 1504.

The Museum of Fine Arts on Heroes' Square is Hungary's largest art museum. Its huge, multi-winged corridors contain Italian, German, Netherlandish and Spanish masterpieces. There are also examples of art from Egypt, Asia Minor, Greece and Rome.

El Greco (1541–1614): *Mary Magdalene,* c. 1580.

Albrecht Dürer (1471–1528):
*Portrait of a Man,* 1500–1510.

City Park is not only the largest park of the city, but thanks to its ancient trees, manicured lawns, flowers, statues and playgrounds, it is the favorite excursion place for the people of Pest and beyond.

The statue symbolizing war on the Millennial Monument.

The Castle of Vajdahunyad, built at the turn of the century, today houses the Museum of Agriculture. It is part of the complex representing the main architectural styles of historical Hungary. The Museum of Agriculture, a hall of which is shown in the inset, has a Baroque façade.

Heroes' Square. In the middle is the column with the representation of Winged Inspiration, with statues of Prince Árpád and his seven chieftains at the base, and in the background, the Millennial Monument celebrating the one thousandth anniversary of the Magyar conquest.

# THE DANUBE

**W**ider rivers and longer rivers cut through the Earth. But there is no other river in the world which connects so many peoples and countries and opens the gate before them to seas and distant continents.

A series of towns drink its water, thousands of industrial works, millions of acres of agricultural land, wells and canals thrive on it.

And it is *living* water: in the summer, bathers, tourists, rowers visit its banks. Near the towns, the banks form an uninterrupted link of boat-houses, weekend houses, resorts. Hiding among the bushes there are little anglers' camps. The surroundings of the quieter backwaters are a genuine anglers' paradise.

It is true, though, that there are no more big sturgeons to be found, and true, the Danube fell a victim to pollution, too, so the "anglers' paradise" must be understood today in the sense that without any particular luck, you may still catch a carp, pike, bream, barbel, or pike-perch.

The Danube belongs to many people, but there has been no people whose fate has been linked with it more closely than our own. It has been the permanent main figure of our history ever since the time the head tribe of the Magyar confederacy settled down near what is the capital today, near the ruined town of Aquincum. In Hungary, the Danube strings together the beads of towns; one can boast of its past, the other of its present. Győr can boast of both.

The "Town of Four Rivers" is a several-thousand-year-old settlement; the rivers Rába and Rábca, and the German name of the town (Raab) recall Arrabona, the Roman name of the town. Győr is often called the capital of the Kisalföld (Little Plain), but its historical role is due above all to its being something of a gateway to the West, lying exactly half-way between Budapest and Vienna. The inner town was no longer new when Napoleon quartered himself among its walls.

Győr is also a fast-developing industrial center, the western outpost of the industrial belt which stretches across northern Hungary. Along the Danube, downstream from Győr, with smoking factory chimneys in the distance, vineyards edge the river. Even Esztergom has some factory chimneys, though it is still more a city of the past; it was the capital of Hungary's first Christian ruler, St. Stephen (1000–1038), and it remained a favorite royal seat of his descendants. Of the medieval palace, only ruins survived the hundred

and fifty years of Turkish rule, but they include the ground floor of St. Stephen's palace in a remarkably intact state. Among the many beauties of Esztergom —library, art gallery, the Cathedral Treasury, the town itself—this almost one-thousand-year-old architectural monument is perhaps the most appealing: the modest residence of the founder of a state.

The river winds lazily between steep mountains, spreading out again near Visegrád, encircling the island of Szentendre and separating into two southward branches.

Visegrád offers many attractions, but seeing them is not enough, you need imagination to discover in the small town of today its historic antecedent: one of the finest, most splendid royal cities of Europe, where any historic monuments that may have chanced to survive the Turkish occupation were destroyed by the Habsburgs.

On the eastern branch of the Danube lies the many-towered town of Vác. On the western branch spreads out the town of irregular shapes, outlines, and rhythms, the paradise of painters, Szentendre. Then in the heart of the country—to complete the anatomical metaphor—the main arteries unite and do not separate again before they reach what was the historic center of Budapest. The next island on its path is the longest—it is industrial Csepel.

Thirty miles further down, the two branches of the river meet again at the spot where a historic present has established a new city; forty years ago there was no trace of it on any map. Its inhabitants are older than the houses they live in or the factories they work in. Although this city, Dunaújváros, was conceived as a whole on the designers' boards, its inhabitants hail from far and wide. In the town registers under the question "place of birth", half the towns and villages of Hungary are listed.

Surrounded by widening swamps and water-logged meadows, the Danube approaches the country's southern border. Many city people would welcome a day or two of the peace, quiet and fresh air which is the year-round right of the stags, deer and wild boar of the Gemenc forests. Guidebooks do not usually mention this rich reserve; wild life, it seems, has to be protected from the disturbance of the lay visitor.

Then comes another historic town, whose very name is synonymous with tragedy: Mohács, where the Turks defeated the Hungarian forces in 1526. Perhaps Hungarian history would indeed have proceeded differently if our troops had outfaced those Turks in the frightening cultic costumes which the inhabitants now don for their annual "busó" festival.

But this life-giving waterway was not the river of death for the first time then—nor for the last. It had to bear the burden of infamy on its back again not long after our great poet Attila József wrote his "By the Danube", which provided the motto to the new history of the peoples of the valley of the Danube.

> The Danube's tender ripples which compose
> Past, present, future, hold each other fast.
> The battle which our ancestors once fought
> Through recollections is resolved in peace,
> And settling at long last the price of thought,
> This is our task, and none too short its lease.
>
> *(Trans. Vernon Watkins)*

Győr, the "city of four rivers", has
been settled for thousands of
years. But its importance to
history was decided by its
proximity to Austria. Its castle
stands on the shores of the Rába.

Marton de Coloswar:
the reliquary of King St. Ladislas
of Hungary, from the second half
of the 14th century. It is displayed
at the Cathedral of Győr,
in the Old Church.

The Bishop's Castle of Győr
was originally built
in the 13th century, though its present
form dates from the 16th century,
when it was modernized.

Esztergom was the seat of St. Stephen, first king of Hungary, and from the 13th century, the center of the Catholic Church. The huge, Neo-Classical structure of its Cathedral, popularly called the Basilica, defines the town's aspect. It is Hungary's largest church. The dome rises one hundred meters above the floor of the crypt below.

The chapel of Tamás Bakócz, archbishop of Esztergom, was built between 1506 and 1511. Its main altar, carved of white Carrara marble, is the work of an Italian master.

The Castle Chapel of the royal palace built during the Age of Árpád in the 12th century.

72

The Christian Museum of Esztergom has a world famous collection of 13th and 14th century Italian art as well as medieval Hungarian panel paintings. Its rare 15th, 16th and 17th century French, Italian and Flemish Gobelins are also well known.

The Master of Garamszentbenedek:
*The Coffin of Our Lord*
(detail), late 15th century.

Follower of Botticelli:
*Enthroned Madonna with the Christ Child,*
late 15th century.

73

The Master M.S.: *The Crucifixion,*
15th–16th centuries.

The Master of Jánosrét:
*The Crucifixion,* 15th–16th centuries.

The Castle Hill of Visegrád, seen from the Danube.

In the 14th century, Visegrád was the permanent residence of the royal court. In the 15th century, King Matthias Corvinus enlarged the palace by the Danube and made it admired for its Renaissance pomp. Today, the city of Visegrád is a favorite holiday resort and excursion place in the Danube Bend.

Detail of the ceremonial courtyard of the royal palace.

The keep of the Lower Castle of Visegrád is known as the Solomon Tower even though Solomon, who conspired against the king, was shut up inside a tower at Visegrád in 1082, while this tower was built only in the 13th century.

Detail of an ornamental fountain from King Matthias's beautiful palace at Visegrád.

80

Detail of the iconostasis
in the Požarevačka Church

Szentendre's Main Square
with the Plague Cross, 1763.

Szentendre, one of the centers for vacationing, excursions
and water sports in the Danube Bend, is beautifully situated and rich in historical protected monuments. The atmosphere is defined by the lovely churches built in the 17th
century by the Serbians who came to settle here. Szentendre is also known as the "town of painters", and its lovely details can be found on the canvases of many outstanding artists.

81

Mardi Gras masquerading at Mohács. Folk tradition among the Sokác who live here, and a tourist attraction: the locals don frightening masks to celebrate the end of Carnival time and the approach of spring.

These trophies are not yet ready for exhibition.

Boar in the woods of Gemenc.

Gemenc is a 20 thousand hectare reservation for animals of the woods, the waters and the fields indigenous to Hungary. There are many boars and various small game, but the major attraction of Gemenc is its holdings of deer, the largest in Europe. Its hunting lodges are always filled to capacity and its permanent exhibition of trophies is the envy of hunters. Its rare birds such as the bald eagle, the black crane and black woodpecker have also made this territory their home.

The black crane is a rare bird.

Gemenc, where game live
protected and undisturbed.

# THE GREAT PLAIN

P oets have always associated the endless plain of the Alföld with freedom, and we have been so influenced by the suggestive effect of their poetic images that we automatically accept them as true.

But let us take a look at Hungarian history: the poetic image that seems to be perhaps fortuitous turns out to have the rigour of law. The Great Plain has been the cradle of all our struggles for freedom and the inexhaustible soil from which every rebellion drew its strength. Even in the darkest centuries, the people of the Hajdú and Cumanian regions and of the Stormy Corner retained something of their independence against the powers that were; they retained their paganism against the Churches, and their human dignity against their lords and masters.

Is the Great Plain beautiful?

We have so often been proud of our faults, and so often ashamed of our virtues, that our self-knowledge is finally reduced to uncertainty; we can no longer value what we are valued for in the world. Yes, the Great Plain—especially the Hortobágy—was once regarded as a tourist attraction, but then we became embarrassed by the *puszta*, the horse-herds and the mirage, and we began to say: we have come a long way from that. Let us look around, at the canals as straight as bowstrings, at the paddy-fields, tractors, pylons, hydroglobes. Yes, we have come a long way from the false romanticism of the ornamented stockwhip and loose-fitting, wide-bottomed trousers.

Our foreign friends come to see us by the thousands and we can hardly dissuade them from seeing the Great Plain, since many of them come just for that. And they remain stubbornly uninterested in the caterpillar tractors, combines and pylons—they can see enough of them at home—but are awed by the horizon fully rounded in every direction, the original *puszta*, the mirage we call *délibáb*. They cannot see it anywhere west of Hungary, at least not in Europe.

Is it boring? But is the sea, only because it is boundless, boring? If the infinity of water is an imposing, dignified sight, why should not the infinity of the earth, fields and gently waving cornfields be so?

To the natives of the Great Plain, the landscape has never appeared monotonous. Indeed, the one-time sea bottom is like a single vast table, and wherever a gentle hillock bulges, it is certain that it was made by people to bury their dead, or that it covers a one-time village. But for those who look carefully at the clouds, the grass, the flowers, this seeming monotony reveals something different—bare sand, fat black soil and sodic soil follow one another, the micro-climate changes, and so do the flora, the architecture, the habits and the taste of the soup.

A foreigner visiting the Great Plain can easily be misled by the appearance of eternal motionlessness, as if the *puszta* had always been so still. Eternal motionlessness? But there is no other part of the country that has changed its image so much in the past centuries—and especially in the last decades.

We have come a long way from the endless sea of swamps, bogs and water-logged fields along the Tisza, where reeds grew six meters high and were once used as vine-props. The Tisza itself is one of the youngest rivers in the world; its present bed is hardly a hundred years old. There was a time when we hurried its flow; now we impede it by canals and barrages. Szeged, the center of the southern part of the country, was built as it stands today hardly a hundred years ago.

And the "eternal" Hortobágy? It is a young and artificial *puszta,* the cemetery of more than fifty villages that were swept away from the surface of the earth without a trace, first by the Turks, then by the floods of the Tisza. The Hortobágy was dried up and has become a *puszta* through the regulation of riverways—and only for a couple of decades. For the "eternal" *puszta* is again changing: it is becoming a crop area before our very eyes.

Continuity has been best preserved by Debrecen, the capital of the Great Plain. A concentrate of its characteristics, Debrecen was several times the birthplace of Hungarian independence, and its greatest value is that it preserves and continues to enrich its historic character.

A *csárda* (tavern)
of the Great Plain.

The Calvinist Great Church is Debrecen's best known historical building. In 1849 and 1945, the National Assembly met here to decide the fate of the country. It is one of the most beautiful examples of Hungarian Neo-Classical architecture. Its organ, installed in 1838, was made by a workshop in Vienna.

The flower carnival in Debrecen.

The bottle dance
at the carnival.

98

The words *csikós, gulyás,* and *puszta,* known throughout the world today, are most aptly represented by the area between the Danube and the Tisza, especially Bugac. Once an exotic area and the symbol of backwardness where the requisites of half-nomadic animal husbandry could easily be found, this aspect of Bugac is moving into its museums. What's left has been preserved for the benefit of tourists.

A *csikós* of Bugac after a tiring *puszta* show.

The "hand-and-five" of Bugac.

99

The other spot related in many ways to the *puszta* is the 115 square kilometers of alkaline and grassy plain known as the Hortobágy, situated in the Great Plain. A real tourist attraction, it is Europe's most famous *puszta*, the home of the *délibáb*, the Hungarian mirage. Even the agriculture which has tamed significant parts of the territory could not hurt either tourism or the *délibáb*.

The *csikós* of Hortobágy at work.

A herd of horses grazing at Hortobágy.

102

The tourist will see domestic animals here which are no longer bred at modern farms. Because they are reared in the open air, these old animal types will make invaluable contributions to gene banks.

The Hungarian gray bull.

A herd of Hungarian gray cattle and a herd of *rackajuh*, a special type of Hungarian sheep.

103

Idyll on the *puszta*.

The most faithful watchdog is the
clever Hungarian sheepdog, the *puli*.

The famous "Nine-Holed" bridge
of the Hortobágy near
the Great Tavern is the country's longest
stone bridge. Surrounded by thick
reeds, it is the home of noisy
water birds.

The Bridge Fair of the Hortobágy, famous far and wide, is held on August 19th and 20th of each year. The vendors bring many useful articles to the fair – and many useless trinkets as well. The ox is roasting over the embers: the *pörkölt* is boiling in the *bogrács*, there is everything one could wish for.

Regions and moods of the Great Plain include not only the *puszta* but the farmsteads and the old village houses as well. It also includes the seemingly endless flat plain and the infinite horizon. Could the men of the Great Plain have received their undaunted yearning for freedom from the huge expanse of space around them?

Hungarian Art Nouveau in the Inner City of Kecskemét.

The "Fancy Palace" of Kecskemét is a good example of Hungarian Art Nouveau.

Kecskemét is the largest town of the region between the Danube and the Tisza. It is also one of the most characteristic towns of the Great Plain. Though it has now gone modern, its traditional city scape is characterized by large, open squares, and its center by Hungarian-style, ornate public buildings.

The Town Hall is the largest and most characteristic public building of the town.

The composer Zoltán Kodály, after whom the famous institute of music is named, was born at Kecskemét. The building housing the institute has been beautifully restored.

The former synagogue built in Moorish style with a Persian onion dome is presently the House of Technology.

The gorgeous painted and embroidered flowers and delicious red paprika of Kalocsa have made her known the world over. The walls of the houses, the porches and softwood furniture are painted by the women, who also embroider fine linen shirts, bodices, head-dresses, aprons, kerchiefs and linen. The paprika is produced by 32 villages of the neighborhood.

The romantic Black House of Szeged was built in 1857.

Most tourists come to Szeged to see the outdoor performances in the summer. The Votive Church, better known as the Dome, has before it a square whose perfect acoustics make it ideal for the Szeged Open-Air Festival. The performances here are attended by six thousand visitors each night.

The New Synagogue of Szeged has unusual and valuable interior decoration. The Arc of the Covenant is made of acacia from the Nile and is decorated with metal mountings. The windows are of stained glass.

# NORTHERN HUNGARY

**B**örzsöny, Cserhát, Mátra, Bükk, the Zemplén Hills, these form the biggest continuous mountain range of the country. Small mountain range of a small country, whose peaks do not figure in the list of important mountains. (Spiked shoes do not sell well in Hungary; the highest peaks can be reached in summer as well as in winter by regular bus services.)

These are mountains of medium height which surround the immense Great Plain; but they emerge from the depths of the one-time sea-bottom with such unexpectedness that often the tourists in walking-shoes are surprised to find that they recall high-altitude climate, air and vegetation.

Sometimes even the clouds—mainly those arriving from the Great Plain—go respectfully round these mini-peaks; the highest summit of the country, the Kékes, which is 1,015 m (3,330 feet) high, is therefore the sunniest place in Hungary.

If our highest mountains are only of modest dimensions, from certain points of view they rank among the first, for example the cave systems at Aggtelek-Jósvafő, where some 22 kilometers (about 14 miles) of galleries have been opened up to now. And the 24-meter "Observatory" of the Baradla cave is the largest stalactite formation in the world.

Or take Tokaj-Hegyalja, the southern foothills of the Zemplén Hills. Here the ancestor of the vine—*Vitis Tokayensis*—appeared already in the tertiary period, much earlier than man's ancestor. And if wine did not appear earlier than man, it is still indigenous to this region. It was here that Attila founded the first city of the Hun Empire; it was here that Árpád and the conquering Magyar tribes first settled and that—according to chronicles—the warriors "drank to celebrate the Conquest" and "went daily inebriated".

Northern Hungary is an interesting example of diversity in homogeneity, of the particular in the general.

Mountainous region—yes; and if we look at the map, it all seems blended. But in reality, how different are the Börzsöny, the Mátra and the Bükk!

This is a historical wine-growing region in general, but which wine connoisseur would confuse the wines of Gyöngyös, Eger and Tokaj-Hegyalja?

It is a traditionally industrial region, but each of its towns has an individual character. Salgótarján is a fast-growing modern industrial city; Eger holds the ghosts of great warriors in the walls of its historic monuments; then comes Miskolc, a spa and also the center of the Borsod industrial region, which in a few decades has developed into the biggest country town. And there are the modern industrial towns which have sprang up around big plants in a few years: Kazincbarcika, Leninváros, etc. And then there is the gem of Hungarian small towns, the family nest of the Rákóczis, the age-old cultural center, Sárospatak.

There is also a great diversity of villages, even within one geographical region. Every one of them is, as it was, a different patch of color; they make up the breathtaking Palots and Matyó regions. But progress has brought civilization, and civilization has turned diversity into uniformity. The girls have cast off their brilliant but uncomfortable and expensive folk costumes in favor of ready-made dresses in the latest fashion.

And villages, too, have slowly cast off their individual character. Hollókő, "the most beautiful of Hungarian villages", is no more today than a sort of reserve; below the old village a new one has been built with those spacious, healthy, but still somehow dismal modern cubic houses, which can be found in new settlements in all parts of the country.

These new houses look alike. The builders want it that way. But a new generation of architects will come with ideas of their own, and the regions will regain their individual character.

The Bükk Mountains in the fall.

128

The Gothic corridor of the Bishop's Palace
in the Castle of Eger,
which was built around 1470.
In September, 1552,
its barely 2 thousand men beat back
the 150 thousand strong Turkish
siege.

The ornate wrought iron gate
of the County Council is the work
of the famous master, Henrik Fazola.
It was made between 1758 and 1761.

The Greek Orthodox church
of Eger, known as the Serbian
Church, has a Byzantine south
Slav interior

129

The Turkish minaret is a popular historical monument of Eger.

Eger, which lies between the Mátra and the Bükk Mountains, is extremely rich in protected historical monuments and well-known for its excellent wines. It is also one of the major tourist attractions of Hungary.

133

The fresco on the main dome of the Archbishop's Cathedral in Eger.

The library of the former Lyceum, today's Teacher Training College of Eger. The fresco by Johann Lucas Kracker represents the synod of Trident. The Lyceum was built between 1763 and 1782.

The Archbishop's Cathedral, popularly called the Basilica, is one of the largest ecclesiastical buildings in the country. It was erected between 1831 and 1836.

134

136

The famous Lipizer horses of Szilvásvárad.

At the Carriage Driving World Championships.

With its waterfalls, trouts, caves, and abundant springs, the valley of the Szalajka is one of the most picturesque regions of the country.

At the stables of Szilvásvárad.

138

Vintage time in Tokaj.

Of all the great wine-producing regions of Hungary, the best known is the 28 villages that make up Tokaj-Hegyalja. Almost every hill produces wine of a unique character, yet wines from here can be easily identified as Tokaj, or Tokay wines. The noble rot which covers the walls of the caves and bottles with its dark velvety coat is a major contributor to the famous taste, especially to the renown of Tokaji Aszú, which has been called "the wine of kings and the king of wines".

Tasting the wine.

The *aszú* grapes are in the bag.

The king of wines – Tokaji Aszú.

In the depths of a cave.

146

The Red Tower in the Rákóczi castle at Sárospatak. The castle was one of the most important headquarters of the Rákóczis. It was especially important in the early 18th century, when Ferenc Rákóczi II led his *kuruc* soldiers in uprising against the Germans. Today, the restored keep, castle, and gardens are a major tourist attraction.

Lake Hámori with the Palace Hotel at Lillafüred.

The stone castle of Diósgyőr was built in the 13th century over an earthen castle dating from the time of the Conquest, in the 10th century. For centuries, it was a peaceful property of the queen which served for amusement and hunting and was mostly spared by bloody sieges. Having been partly restored, it is today one of the major surviving relics of medieval Hungary.

147

The colorful headdress
of the Palóc is worn today only
on very special occasions.

Beautifully situated Hollókő
is known as the loveliest village
in the country. Rich in folk art
and tradition, the twenty or so houses
around its small 16th century
wooden-towered church have
become a Palóc "folk reservation".
Hollókő differs from
open-air folk museums in that
the buildings here have remained
in their original places, and some
of them are still inhabited. In 1987,
UNESCO added Hollókő to its
prestigeous list of the world's
cultural heritage.

The children of Hollókő.

Small-talk: folk costumes are still
worn during holidays on
Palócföld, the land of the Palóc
– and for the sake of the tourists
and their inquisitive cammeras.

Our mountains and forests are inhabited areas; compared to other parts of the world, they are "domesticated" forests, and "domesticated" hills; those that fall at some distance from our homes we still visit on the weekends. We have neither wildernesses, jungles, nor blood-thirsty beasts of prey; nature in Hungary has accommodated herself to Man. Though she steers clear of the towns, if we open the door to her in the villages, she sneaks right in.

Coal burner in the Mátra Mountains with the charcoal kiln in the background.

The Bükk Mountains in autumn and winter.

# TRANSDANUBIA

**F**or the West, Hungary is an Eastern country, for the East, it is more or less a Western one. In reality we are neither. Or if you like, we are both at the same time. This spiritual schizophrenia has grown from a historical duality rooted in the country's peculiar situation. It is a beneficial, in fact *realistic* schizophrenia. West of the Danube, ethnographical, geographical and climatic similarities are indeed more striking with the West, while east of the Tisza, they are more pronounced with the East.

The Hungarians appeared in Transdanubia only five hundred years after the collapse of the province of Pannonia, and the vestiges of Roman civilization certainly influenced the decision of the majority of the Hungarians to settle here. Later it was here, too, that the Church built most of its strongholds.

This undulating, forest-clad land is the oldest cultured area of the country, where the greatest number of monuments can be found today. To tell the truth, they are mostly in ruin. When it comes to ruins, we are unbeatable. The once lively phrase, "not a stone was left standing," has become an absolute commonplace in the Hungarian language.

A globe-trotter in a Venetian gallery will easily compare the Piazza San Marco of a five-hundred-year-old *veduta* painting with the real one just outside the window. And if he happens to be a Hungarian, he suddenly feels the meaning of that phrase with full force, and marvels at the idea that stones have been left standing for five or six hundred years.

At that time, in the golden age of Venice, the Hungarian king, Matthias Corvinus, was one of the most powerful monarchs in Europe, and his contemporaries sang the praises of his magnificent palaces at Visegrád and Buda. And what is left of these? If archeologists unearth a carved stone or two they are delighted to build around it in their imagination the splendid palace worthy of Matthias's rank, power and wealth.

Several hundred castles were built on the territory of historical Hungary, and a fair number have remained on the country's present-day territory. However, only one has remained relatively intact: the castle at Siklós. The rest were more or less radically destroyed either in consecutive wars or in times of peace. The latter, premeditated destruction, was brought about in order that anti-Habsburg rebellion should not raise its ugly head, and was particularly radical.

Who could blame the inhabitants of the neighborhood if they used the stones of destroyed castles, palaces and monasteries? The ruins of the palace of Visegrád were also used for a long time as a quarry by the German settlers, and not without encouragement from high quarters where it was argued that if the past of a nation was eliminated, it would perish by itself.

Of course, historic monuments are scarce in Transdanubia only in comparison to how many there *could be*. At Sopron and Kőszeg, for example, there still are quite a few. These two former border fortresses, today holiday resorts, are practically open-air museums. For centuries Sopron has been the western gate of the country, and has always felt Western influences, positive or negative, in the most direct way. In spite of this—or perhaps because of this—it represents best the character and patriotism of our historic towns.

At Szombathely the 2000-year-old Roman past is felicitously combined with the present. This is the natural center of western Transdanubia. The "capitals" of the different regions are being created in the same manner: Veszprém, as the center of the Bakony Mountains; Tatabánya, a town which will soon unite four settlements, as that of the neighboring coalfields; Nagykanizsa, as the center of the oil-fields of Zala County. Székesfehérvár's development is due rather to traffic: the one-time residence of the Árpád dynasty is today the busiest cross-road of Transdanubia. Rich in historic monuments, the vestiges of its golden age are to be found mostly in the Garden of Ruins—few vestiges if we consider the fact that 37 Hungarian kings were crowned and 17 buried in this town.

Pécs is to Transdanubia what Debrecen is to the region beyond the Tisza: the quintessence of its characteristic features, a summary of its historic and cultural traditions. It is not centrally situated, but its future is assured for centuries to come by coal and uranium mined from the neighboring Mecsek Mountains.

The Mecsek Mountains are quite a special element in the Hungarian climate: it is here that the average yearly temperature is the highest, and that the northern wind is felt the least; spring arrives and flowers bloom first here. This region is the stronghold of Mediterranean climate, just as western Transdanubia is that of wet, balanced subalpine climate, and the Great Plain that of the less moderate Continental one. Transdanubia is rich in medicinal baths and thermal springs, too—as almost every part of the country. In the Hungarian basin the earth's crust is less thick and the temperature produced by magma heat is much greater than elsewhere. Many towns are becoming modern places of pilgrimage on account of the medicinal baths: their composition, their variety and their frequent occurrence are truly unique.

Transdanubian fields after harvest.

For centuries, Sopron has been the gate to Hungary. Despite this fact – or perhaps because of it – the town is the best representative of patriotism in the country.

Folk-Baroque ornamentation on a house in Szent Mihály utca, built in 1710.

The Benedictine Church, better known as the Goat Church, is one of the main protected monuments of Sopron. Built in the 13th century, its tower, decorated with Gothic lace pattern, is from the 14th century.

Templom utca with the Fire Tower, the symbol of Sopron, in the background. Though its foundation is from the Roman Age, it was built only during the rule of the Árpáds. The centuries have left the stamp of their predominant styles on the tower: at the bottom it is Romanesque, in the middle Renaissance, and at top, it is Baroque.

One of the consoles of the Chapter Hall in the former Franciscan monastery in Templom utca, built in the 14th century.

The medieval house built in 1480 at Új utca 16 forms part of the ancient network of houses that give Sopron its special character.

The yard with loggia at Templom utca 2 is just one example of the architectural style that we admire so much today.

Façade of the Eszterházy Mansion at Templom utca 2. Today it is the home of the Museum of Mining.

164

Courtyard of the Fabricius House at Főtér 6. In its basement have been found remnants of a Roman Age floor heating system from the 4th century. Today, the house has been turned into a museum.

165

The Esterházy Palace of Fertőd is known as the "Hungarian Versailles". It is a huge complex built by Prince Miklós Esterházy in the middle of the 18th century. It had a permanent theater and opera, whose court conductor between 1761 and 1790 was Joseph Haydn. The 126-room castle was heavily damaged during the Second World War, but has since been restored. Today its reception room and garden are the scene of concerts once again.

Details that complete the beauty of the "Hungarian Versailles".

Jurisics Square in Kőszeg has
kept its 17th century aspect to this
day. This is a quaint world of
much charm, the stone structures,
old dwelling houses and churches
have preserved the atmosphere
of past centuries. In this "outdoor
museum", the later, Baroque
additions to the town strike us as
"modern".

The saw-toothed placement
of the houses in Kőszeg are the result
of military considerations.

The slender, onion-domed St. Anne's Church was built in the early 17th century on medieval foundations.

Heroes' Gate, built to commemorate the four hundredth anniversary of the Turkish siege, has also preserved the mood of former times. Today, it has become the symbol of Kőszeg. Memorial plaques commemorating the former guardians of the town, the Hungarian Jacobins and the heroic dead of the First World War line the walls under the arcades.

The coat of arms of the city of Kőszeg in its original form at the 15th century City Council.

177

The 13th century Abbey Church of Ják, which has one nave, two isles and two towers, is a masterpiece of Árpád Age architecture. Its Romanesque main gate is the most ornate in the country. Built by the Benedictines as an abbey monastery, both its impressive exterior and interior carved and painted decorations and well balanced proportions make it one of the most beautiful examples of monastic churches built by a family.

178

Szombathely, known in the Roman age as Savaria, is the financial and intellectual center of Western Transdanubia. It was founded by the Romans in the middle of the 1st century along the Amber Route which connected the Baltic Sea and the Mediterranean. It developed into one of the major towns of the Roman province of Pannonia, and kept this prestige for many centuries.

Funerary tablet from the Roman Age.

The ancient Amber Route.

Bas-reliefs of the Roman Age.
Temple of Isis.

The single nave, early Gothic, single towered village church of Velemér is a beautiful example of late 13th century ecclesiastical architecture.

184

The frescoes of the church of Velemér were painted in 1378 by János Aquila.

185

As traditional village life vanishes, appreciation of its material requisites grows. We are just beginning to appreciate the beauty, atmosphere, and deeply human qualities of the objects, architecture and landscape of rural Hungary.

An old water mill at Göcsej.

Interior of a village house from Zala.

Peasant house in the outdoor village museum.

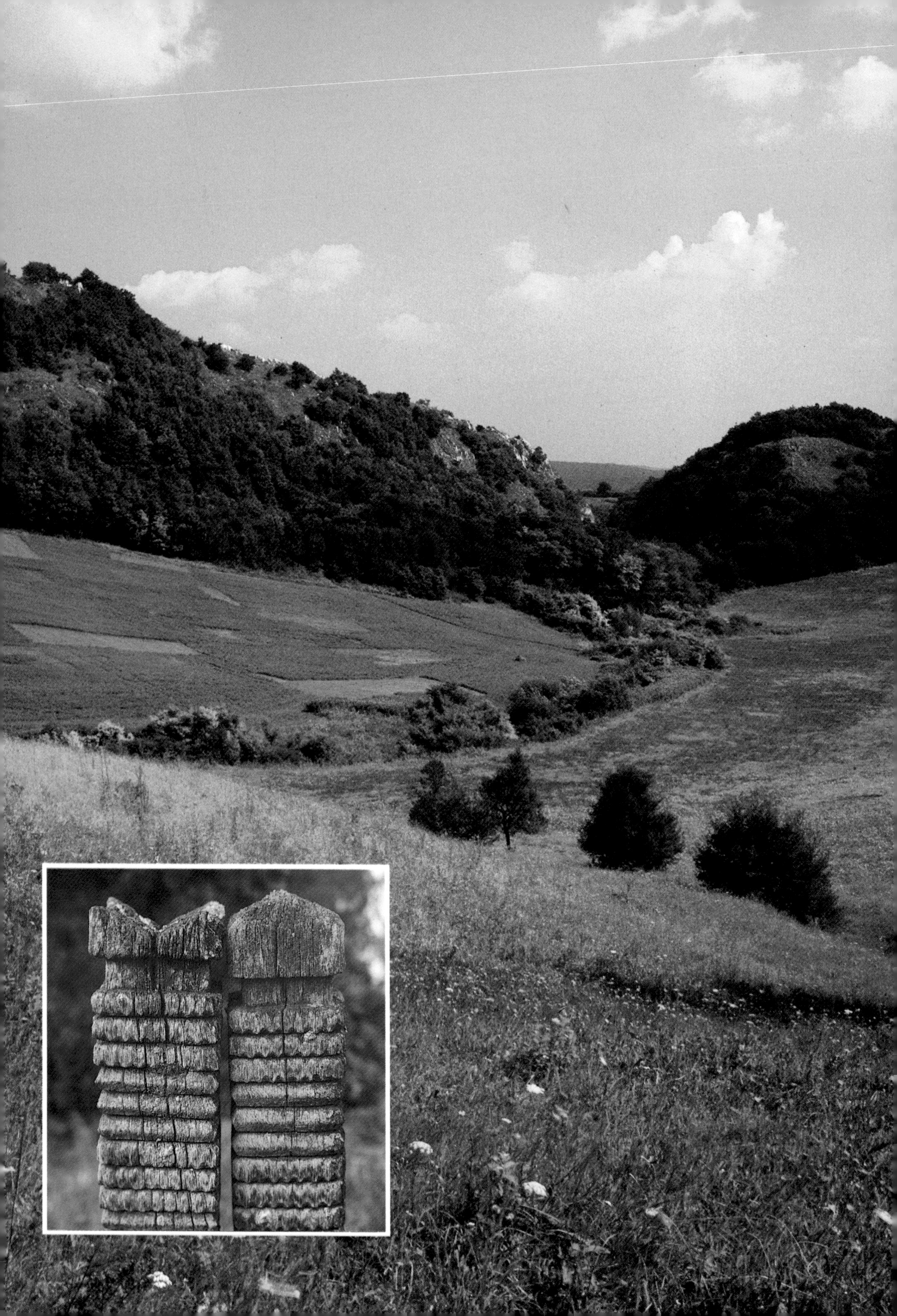

Őrség, the westernmost region of the country, is of special interest both ethnographically and historically. The border area settled after the Conquest developed unique customs, life-styles and forms of settlement, and has preserved its privileges throughout the centuries.

An Őrség landscape. Inset: wooden headposts of a man and wife.

A chapel in the Őrség.

Roadside crucifix.

St. Peter's Cathedral dates from the reign of King St. Stephen in the early 11th century. Its present shape is the result of many alterations.

The interior of the Cathedral

Pécs, the unofficial capital of Southern Transdanubia, is the influential junction of the country's public administration, industry, transportation, commerce and culture. Its historical role stretched way back to before the time of the Conquest. It has been inhabited since time immemorial, and its past as a city goes back two thousand years.

The minaret of the Yakovali Hassan *djami*.

The *djami* of Pasha Gazi Khasim was built at the end of the 16th century. Today it is the Inner City Parish Church.

Interior of the Gazi Khasim *djami*.

Tivadar Csontváry Kosztka (1853–1919): *Storm on the Great Hortobágy*, 1903.

198

199

Csontváry: *The Waterfalls of Jajce*, 1903.

Pécs is a city of many fine
museums. Of these,
the Csontváry Museum and
the Vasarely Museum, found
in the house where the artist
was born, are among the most
frequently visited by lovers
of 20th century art.

Victor Vasarely (b.1908): *Vega – Chess*, 1961.

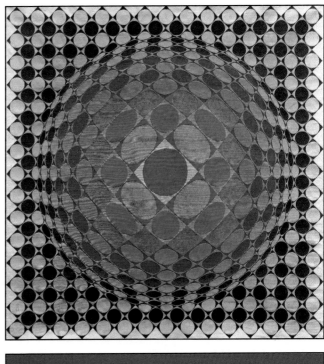

201

In the Vasarely Museum.

202

Victor Vasarely: *Teries*, 1972–1974.

The painted choir and wooden coffered ceiling of the Calvinist church of Szenna, from 1785.

St. Stephen's Chapel of Mecseknádasd, built in the 13th century.

The castle of Siklós is the only intact structure of its kind in the country. Built in the 14th century, it was inhabited through the ages, and is still inhabited today. It is a hotel, tourist hostel and restaurant. The curtain arch shaped windows of the chapel are from the 15th century.

The Abbey of Pannonhalma is the main monastery of Hungarian Benedictines. Founded by Prince Géza in 996, it was built by his son King St. Stephen. Its chapel was consecrated in 1001. Many things have been added to it since, and many things have fallen to ruin, but it is nevertheless one of the richest complexes of historical relics in the country.

209

The 50-meter high "New Tower"
which crowns the Pannonhalma
complex was built between 1829
and 1832. Its 13th century crypt,
a mixture of Roman and early
Gothic styles, is enhanced by
consoles in the shape of heads.

In the medieval section of the
monastery, the Gothic cloister
is enhanced by carved consoles.
Next to one of these, the date
1486, when the cloister was built,
is clearly visible.

# LAKE BALATON

**A** country as small as Hungary should have a sea to match. Indeed, in just a few hours you can drive around the 600 square kilometer (232 square mile) "Hungarian sea," as Lake Balaton has been called for almost two centuries, perhaps not quite without foundation. For it should be appreciated if a small country, far from any ocean, produces a boundless stretch of water which, if seen from a certain angle and preferably in misty weather, cannot be told apart from a real sea. It is another matter that many people are misled by this nickname.

Those for instance, who do not take it seriously. "This wash-tub?" they shrug scornfully, like veteran sailors, when they are warned of the approach of a storm. These scornful sea-dogs represent quite a considerable proportion of those who find a watery grave in Lake Balaton. The storm rushing down on the lake from the Bakony Mountains with terrifying force does not respect even the most genuine sailors, and the Balaton's waves—precisely because of the shallowness of the lake—are much more abrupt, and thus more dangerous, than sea waves.

But those who take it seriously are also easily misled by the nickname "Hungarian sea". They make comparisons and references, they never tire of making plans for the future of the lake, and would like to transform the shores of Lake Balaton into a kind of substitute for the French Riviera.

To be truthful, the Balaton is a poor imitation of a sea. But its individuality consists precisely in characteristics which no seaside—not even the Côte d'Azur—would match. Take, for instance, its shallowness. Its water warms up easily, and especially the water near the shores. Even small waves bring up from the bottom the fine grains of mud and this, the experts say, gives the water a certain curative effect. This shallowness also makes possible the dazzling play of colors—and many other things, too.

The Somogy shore in its full 70-kilometer length (44 miles) is a marvellous, huge children's beach where they can bathe, row and play without danger several hundred meters—at some places even a kilometer—from the shore. In this respect the more distinguished sea with its salty, colder water, with its more abrupt shores and unforeseeable dangers is out of the question as a rival, but no other freshwater beach is larger or more suitable for children than the southern shore of the Balaton with its soft water. The hundreds of thousands of families with children who come here regularly appreciate not having to keep a constant watch on their children as they play in the sands or splash about in the water.

Lake Balaton is relatively young: geologists estimate that it is no more than twenty thousand years old. The northern shore is much more varied, and it was here that the first holiday resorts, such as Balatonfüred, Tihany, Badacsony, Keszthely and Hévíz, were built. Here the shore offers so many sights that no holiday is long enough to take them all in; it always passes too quickly.

On the northern shore, the centrally situated Tihany peninsula is particularly interesting. It is a rich museum of natural and historic sights and one of the major nature conservation areas of the country. An ancient castle, Avar mounds, cells hollowed out in the rocks by monks, remind us of the past. One of the earliest written records of the Hungarian language was found here in the crypt of the Abbey.

And from here, from the top of the hills of the Tihany peninsula, we can see how the shore of the lake is becoming a single settlement. On clear summer evenings it is one long string of lights. The time is not far off when one of the most singular and largest cities of the world will spring to life here with a pool the size of the Hungarian sea in the middle, bordered by a densely populated 200-kilometer High Street running along its shore—and sometimes more vacationers than it can hold.

The vulcanic hills of the Balaton region.

The pier at Balatonfüred dressed up for a big race. The Tihany Peninsula, Hungary's foremost natural conservation area, is the most popular tourist spot on Lake Balaton. It is also one of the most frequented vacation places.

The ample literature on the lake has so far ignored one of the special aspects of its waters: along a 70-kilometer stretch of its southern shore, its waters make Europe's safest – and largest – playground for children.

Getting ready for a surfing race.

Grapevines at the foot of Somló Hill, the smallest of the country's outstanding wine producing regions, though by no means the least important. Like the Badacsony Mountains, the basic rock of the hill is basalt, while the lava remains covering the basalt are similar to the lava of Mount Vesuvius.

Its health institutions, summer places, unique natural endowments and the curative effects of its thermal springs have made Hévíz an internationally known health resort.

Winter on Lake Balaton:
the pier at Tihany.

The former Festetics Castle
of Keszthely is the largest and most
significant cultural building
of the Balaton region. Its old wing
houses the invaluable volumes
of the Helikon Library.

A view of Tihany with the Inner Lake
a fisherman's paradise
Its water level is 25 meters higher
than the Balaton

The organ of the Abbey Church
of Tihany was made
in the 18th century.

The Abbey Church seen from
the village. Its present Baroque
shape, with the adjoining
monastery, dates
from 1719–1745, when it was
rebuilt from the stones of the
castle of Tihany, destroyed
by the imperial troops of Austria

The Crypt was built in the mid-11th
century, when the abbey
was founded. Andreas I,
the founder of the abbey, was
buried here in 1060. Its deed
of foundation from 1055 is the first
written record of the Hungarian
language.

Folk-Baroque press house
on St. George Hill.

Riding school at Pécsely. Tourists
who come to this Upper Balaton
township will also enjoy
the nature conservation area on
its outskirts, as well as the castle
ruins and look-out tower.

Wine cellar at Aszófő, the "neck" of the Tihany Peninsula.

The excellent Hungarian cuisine also attracts many guests. A popular *csárda*, or Hungarian-style restaurant, is found at Vámos, in the Upper Balaton region. All around the shores of the lake, the summer population exceeds the local populations many times. As a result, life and recreation around the lake have accommodated themselves to the requirements of tourists and vacationers.

230

Veszprém, the "capital of th
Bakony", is rich in historic.
monuments. The first Hungaria
bishopric was founded here in th
last millennium. The castle wa
built on a dolomite clif
The 13th century wall painting
representing the Apostles (inse
are in the Gizella Chape

Ruins of the Pauline monastery
and church of Nagyvázsony,
founded by Kinizsi in 1483.

The medieval Kinizsi Castle c
Nagyvázsony was bestowed upo
Pál Kinizsi, the legendar
commander who fought agains
the Turks, by King Matthias

231

Sailing on the ice on Lake Balaton.

Fishermen's boats and smacks are ever-present props of life on the lake. At dawn and sunset, fishermen by the thousands come to the lakeshore, the piers and fishing stages to wait patiently for a catch. If it doesn't come, they tend to blame the professional fishermen with their mile-long nets, who won't leave anything for them.

## Photography

Cover photo: Árpád Patyi
Back-cover photo: János Eifert
Imre Baric: 7, 9, 27, 38
Lóránt Bérczi: 31, 50, 51, 68, 70, 71, 230
Lajos Czeizing: 134, 135
Tamás Díner: 33
János Eifert: 6, 53, 113, 144, 157, 220, 221, 222, 234
István Faragó: 49, 79, 200
György Gara: 4, 8, 21, 30
András Hász: 2, 5, 22, 40, 41, 45, 69, 78, 85, 94, 126, 159, 163, 164, 167, 178, 222, 223, 236
Károly Hemző: 12, 24, 25, 26, 28, 34, 35, 43, 46, 47, 52, 61, 77, 92, 95, 96, 97, 101, 103, 108, 109, 114, 120, 121, 136, 140, 141, 142, 148, 150, 176, 213, 214, 216, 219, 227, 228, 229, 235, 237
Róbert Horling (MTI): 123, 124
Tibor Hortobágyi: 131, 139, 146, 153
György Kapocsy: 91, 98, 99, 100, 102, 105, 110, 111
Péter Korniss: 32, 44, 59, 84, 104, 106, 107, 149, 151, 152
Ákos Kürti (MTI): 143
László Mészáros: 65, 83, 87, 88, 89, 155
István Panyik: 147, 193, 194, 197
Árpád Patyi: 29, 60, 62, 64, 80, 93, 112, 127, 138, 156, 166, 170, 174, 180, 184, 186, 187, 188, 191, 218
Csaba Raffael (MTI): 10
Endre Rácz: 66, 67, 90, 116, 122, 125, 160, 161, 162, 168, 169, 171, 173, 177, 179, 182, 183, 185, 190, 192, 195, 196, 203, 204, 205, 206, 207, 208, 209, 210, 211, 212, 215, 225, 226
Tamás Révész: 181
Herbert Saphier: 39
Alfréd Schiller: 15, 16, 17, 18, 19, 20, 54, 55, 56, 57, 58, 198, 199, 201, 202
József Szabó: 217
Zsolt Szabóky: 1, 3, 11, 13, 23, 36, 37, 42, 48, 63, 76, 128, 129, 130, 132, 133, 137, 145, 154, 224
Károly Szelényi: 14, 72, 73, 74, 75, 189, 231, 233
János Szerencsés: 86, 158, 165
Gyula Tahin: 81, 82, 115, 117, 118, 119, 172, 175, 232

Essay translated by Tünde Vajda
Captions and practical information
translated by Zsuzsa Béres
Design by Julianna Rácz

© Essay: Gyula Fekete
ISBN 963 13 3455 4

Second edition

Printed in Hungary, 1991
KNER Printing House, Békéscsaba